Pandas Are Bears, Not Cats!

Edited by Li Chaodong   **Translated by** Xuemeng Angela Li, Daniel Jingyuan Ni

HOHAI UNIVERSITY PRESS

ROYAL COLLINS
Books Beyond Boundaries

There are many fascinating animals on Earth: penguins, kangaroos, Arctic hares, blue-footed boobies...

Pandas, the "national treasure" of China, are obviously one of the most loved ones among them.

Pandas are born with big, bright eyes surrounded by sunglasses-like dark circles.

They are chubby, fluffy, and lovable.

Pandas are known for their pigeon-toed walking style and sharp claws.

Giant pandas have lived on Earth for at least 8 million years. The Chinese discovered giant pandas early on and called them with many interesting names: spotted bear, white bear, iron-eating beast, black and white bear, spot-headed bear, Chinese bear, bamboo bear …

In 1869, French missionary Armand David captured a bamboo bear. Unfortunately, the bear died before he was able to bring it back to France. David then made a specimen out of the bear's skin with deep regret.

When the specimen was exhibited in the Sichuan Beibei Museum in 1939, it was introduced as "Mao Xiong" ("cat bear" in Chinese, where Mao stands for cat and Xiong stands for bear).

At the time, the Chinese were accustomed to reading texts from right to left. Thus, they called it "Xiong Mao" (bear cat), which has become the official Chinese name for pandas since then.

Although the Chinese name (Xiong Mao) for pandas has the word "cat" (mao) in it, pandas are not a member of the Felidae (cat) family, but the Ursidae (bear) family instead!

Let's meet the members of the big Ursidae family together.

We have black bears who love to feed on honey and plants.

The brown bear, who enjoys berries, meat, and salmon, is also a member of the family.

We also have the spectacled bear who likes to eat bromeliads and occasionally feed on meat.

Here is the polar bear, who lives in the Arctic and normally feeds on seals.

A long time ago, the ancestors of pandas also enjoyed eating meat. They were even able to hunt down deer for food by collaborating with each other.

One day, the temperature plummeted unexpectedly. The whole world almost turned into a huge icehouse.

Many animals that lived in north China couldn't stand the continuous snowstorms and died one after another. Animals that survived were forced to migrate to the warmer southern regions.

Thus, the ancestors of pandas had to compete with the newcomers for meat, but they lost the competition due to their smaller figures. To survive, they started feeding on wild berries and grasses.

But how did they survive the winter when berries and grasses were gone?

Luckily, they eventually found an amazing plant—bamboo. It sprouts from bamboo shoots in the spring, grows into bamboo around summer, and doesn't rot even during the winter.

And that's how they gained access to food all year round!

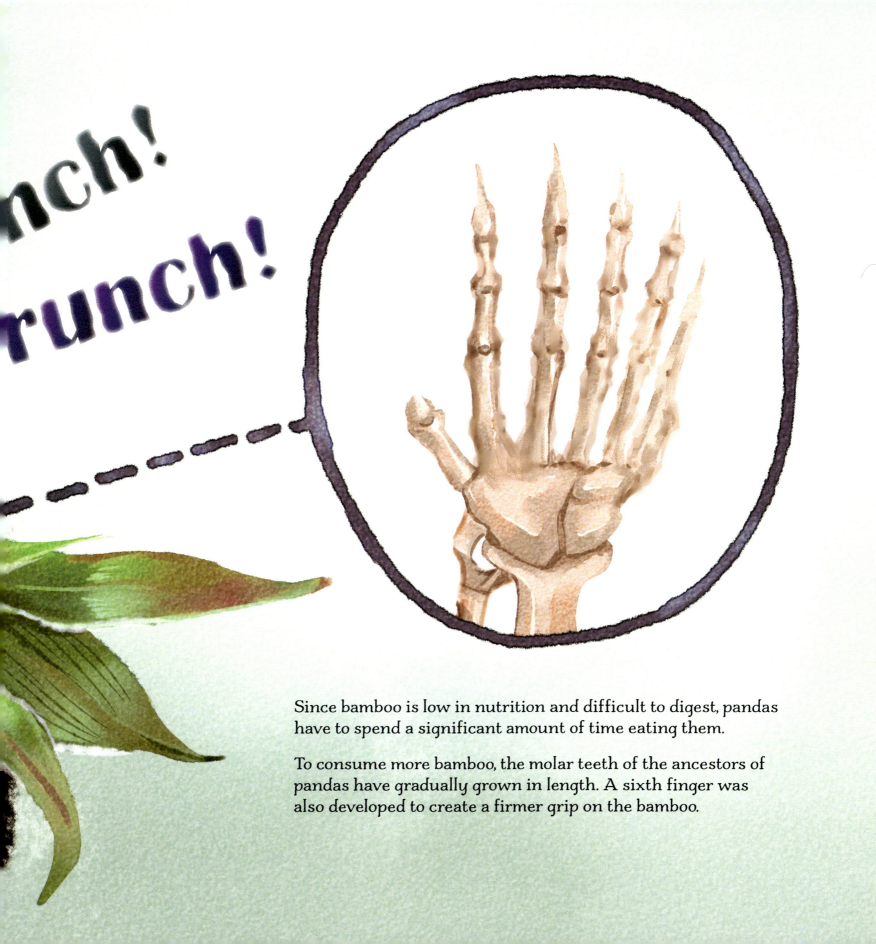

Since bamboo is low in nutrition and difficult to digest, pandas have to spend a significant amount of time eating them.

To consume more bamboo, the molar teeth of the ancestors of pandas have gradually grown in length. A sixth finger was also developed to create a firmer grip on the bamboo.

Nowadays, pandas still face numerous life crises and are extremely low in quantity.

Due to insufficient nutrition and the limited quantity of bamboo, wild pandas can only live up to about 20 years old, but captive-bred ones can survive until about 30 years old.

Female pandas can only conceive once a year for an average of two to three days.

Mother pandas' birth time is flexible. For example, when food sources are scarce, they will keep their babies in them a bit longer.

Mother pandas will spend 1.5 years or sometimes even 2 years taking care of their babies until the birth of the next one.

Newborn baby pandas

1–2 weeks old

Newborn baby pandas are extremely tiny, weighing only one-thousandth of their mother's weight. They can only survive with delicate care from their mothers.

1 month old

3 months old

Normally, mother pandas who give birth to twin pandas cannot take good care of both at the same time. So, they will focus on raising the stronger cub, making it difficult for the weaker one to survive.

To protect pandas, China has established natural reserves for them.

Although pandas are attractive for their cute appearance, they are essentially carnivorous animals. Unlike the breeder, you should be careful when getting in close contact with them.

In addition to establishing natural reserves, the environmental protection department has also sent some pandas to zoos for breeding.

Nowadays, pandas are increasingly growing in quantity and are not seen as an endangered species anymore. However, they are still categorized as a vulnerable species due to external factors such as environmental impact.

Since the Tang Dynasty (AD 618–907), pandas have become the "diplomats" of China. They were delivered to numerous countries and can still be seen in many.

Country	Zoo
USA	Zoo Atlanta
USA	Smithsonian National Zoological Park
Mexico	Chapultepec Zoo
Spain	Zoo Aquarium de Madrid
Austria	Schönbrunn Zoo
Germany	Zoo Berlin
Thailand	Chiang Mai Zoo
Japan	Adventure World in Shirahama, Wakayama
Japan	Ueno Zoo
Japan	Kobe Oji Zoo
Australia	Adelaide Zoo

Besides establishing protection measures, experts have also been continuously conducting research on pandas. For example, they have been trying to figure out whether humans can eat and digest bamboo one day, just like pandas, if abundant food sources are no longer available.

Pandas are highly recognizable because of their distinctive black-and-white colors. Their cute postures always leave people around the world with deep impressions.

Because of that, pandas were selected as the symbol of WWF (World Wide Fund for Nature).

Since then, led by pandas, many more animals have been taken under protection.

Pandas Are Bears, Not Cats!

Edited by Li Chaodong
Translated by Xuemeng Angela Li and Daniel Jingyuan Ni

First published in 2024 by Royal Collins Publishing Group Inc.
Groupe Publication Royal Collins Inc.

Headquarters: 550-555 boul. René-Lévesque O Montréal (Québec)
H2Z1B1 Canada
America office: 122 Eugenia Ave, San Francisco, CA 94110

Original edition © Hohai University Press

All rights reserved. Without limiting the rights under copyright reserved above, no part of this publication may be reproduced, stored in or introduced into a retrieval system, or transmitted in any form or by any means (electronic, mechanical, photocopying, recording, or otherwise), without the prior written permission of both the copyright owner and the above publisher of this book.

ISBN: 979-8-9852490-1-9

To find out more about our publications,
please visit www.royalcollins.com.